IN THE
WORKPLACE

Sport AND Leisure

GEOFF BARKER

Evans

Contents

Working in the Sport and Leisure Industry   6

Chapter 1   **Sports Roles**   8

Chapter 2   **Leisure Centre Work**   16

Chapter 3   **The Great Outdoors**   24

Chapter 4   **Sport and Leisure Tuition**   30

Chapter 5   **Sport and Leisure Development**   38

Further Information   44

Glossary   45

Index   46

Working in the Sport and Leisure Industry

Sport and leisure is a changing and growing industry with a wide range of careers for enthusiastic young people. The sector covers sport, recreation, health and fitness, and includes administrative positions as well as sportier indoor and outdoor activities.

BIG BUSINESS

Public and private organisations profit from people's continuing interest in sport and active leisure. Sportswear, such as designer T-shirts, trainers and replica tops may simply be fashionable accessories for many people, but it also reflects our obsession with sport today. We are interested in our own health and fitness, so there is the desire, though not always the will-power, to exercise and get fit. Most of us are aware of the importance that sport and active leisure play in a healthy mind and body.

The sport and leisure sector provides activities that everyone can enjoy, no matter what age or level of ability.

Working in the sport and leisure industry can be a very positive choice – the job encourages you to think healthily all the time.

SPORTING STARS

This book gives a representative sample of the types of professions available in the industry. Professional sportsmen and women who have the talent and determination to reach the top make up a relatively small number compared with those involved in the sport and active leisure sector generally. As well as the athletes, cyclists, footballers, golfers, jockeys, skaters, squash players and swimmers, there are thousands of jobs in health and sports clubs, leisure centres, horse riding and trekking clubs, outdoor activity centres and gyms. There are also dedicated individuals who coach or instruct others in their favourite sports, disciplines or exciting outdoor activities.

FRESH OPPORTUNITIES

As sporting organisations work with local authorities to get the public active and enthusiastic about keeping fit, there are an increasing number of opportunities in sport and leisure administration. Sports development officers provide young people with opportunities for enjoyable sporting and leisure activities. They see the benefits for local communities – with more motivated youngsters and a reduction in crime rates. Sports promotion and marketing opportunities are also on the increase. As more people become interested in sport, media coverage grows around the world. In the past, we relied on sports pages in newspapers, and radio reports, for sporting news. Now, when we want to know who has won a tie-break in tennis or who has just scored a vital goal in a football relegation battle, we're probably watching the game live on satellite TV or online on computers or mobile phones. People will pay to watch the best sports stars play and there'll be a huge team of journalists, reporters, camera people and men and women behind the scenes to bring the latest pictures and stories to you.

HANDY HINT
If you want to work in sport and leisure, you do not necessarily have to be an active participant, but you should have a strong interest in the industry. It is likely that you are interested in sport, and you're probably passionate about it! If you're enthusiastic, have good communication skills, and are happy being part of a team, as well as a good potential leader, then this might be the right field for you.

Sports Roles

Most of us can only dream of sporting success. Those with genuine talent are usually spotted young, before leaving school. But you don't have to be a professional sportsperson to take advantage of the hundreds of careers open to you in sport and leisure.

SPORTSMEN AND WOMEN

With sports, there are certainly plenty of careers to choose from. Team sports include basketball, cricket, football, field and ice hockey. Individual sports include athletics, cycling, golf, horse-racing, swimming and tennis. Gradually, the number of women participating in traditionally male-dominated sports is increasing. Disabled athletes have more opportunities to shine than ever before, with the pinnacle of achievement being the four-yearly Paralympics.

SUPPORTING ROLES

If you enjoy playing sports, the chances are you will always be an amateur. It is great to aim for the top, but it is also important to take a realistic approach. Apart from professional players and athletes, there are other jobs within the sports industry which support the individual sport or discipline, from horse-racing to tennis and from hockey to rugby. There are officiating roles, such as umpires and referees, as well as other jobs including agents, talent scouts, stable hands, golfing caddies and groundspeople. Although there is a wide range of jobs, there is considerable competition for the relatively few openings at the top of each sport.

TO BECOME A FOOTBALLER, YOU WILL NEED

●

talent and a desire to succeed

●

self-discipline

●

dedication and will-power

MAIN TASKS – FOOTBALLER

●

training as hard as possible

●

practising skills

●

getting your game plan right

●

handling pressure at big games

●

working on strength and conditioning

●

focusing on diet and lifestyle

Serena Williams is one of the tennis greats. Hugely talented, she has worked on her game with a strong, singleminded focus.

Aspiring footballers can look to David Beckham as a role model, but life is tough at the top.

Ian – footballer

'When I was 13 or 14, I didn't really have a clue what I wanted to be. I loved playing football, and to do what you love and get paid for it is great. My dad had played professional football, and at nine years old I joined my first football team. There were other players who were as good as me, but I was always out practising . . . and as you play for youth teams it's a bigger environment with better players, and you keep improving.

'I'd always hoped to play for my home town team, and I had my first professional contract with them at 19. There's nothing better than playing in front of a big crowd on match day – if you score a goal you just hear the roar of crowd. There's nothing quite like it.

'You have to be disciplined. On Friday nights your mates are all going out, but you have to look after yourself to play on Saturday. It's also difficult sometimes if you pick up an injury. We'd got to the cup final and I'd scored a few goals on the way, but I knew I wasn't fit for the final itself. I had to miss that and the chance never came again. That's tough.'

A sports physiotherapist is a trusted adviser to many sportsmen and women. Here tennis professional Mary Pierce is treated for an injury on the side of the court.

ROAD TO RECOVERY

Professional sportsmen and women try hard to keep themselves at the peak of physical condition – after all, their livelihoods depend upon it. However, every sportsperson will get an injury at sometime or other during their sporting career. Injuries are more likely to be frequent in contact sports. Physiotherapists and other skilled professional therapists, such as massage practitioners, can work with sportsmen and women to deal with injuries and set their clients back on the road to recovery as quickly as possible.

SPORTS PHYSIOTHERAPIST

Sports physiotherapists work in a variety of settings – from leisure centres and health and fitness clubs to clinics treating sports injuries, and sports clubs. Therapists diagnose and treat all sorts of injuries, at all sporting levels, from amateur to professional. As well as an ability to use their hands effectively in massage and manipulation, sports physiotherapists need good counselling skills. They may need to encourage and motivate frustrated sportsmen and women at difficult times to persuade them to carry on and work hard with their treatment and rehabilitation.

MAIN TASKS – SPORTS PHYSIOTHERAPIST

●

assessing a client's injury

●

treating a client's injury

●

preparing a management programme

●

planning and maintaining a schedule of work

●

supervising exercise

Liang – sports physiotherapist

'I was lucky enough to have a successful sports career in my twenties, but I knew that wouldn't last forever . . . so I decided to become a physiotherapist. The training is hard . . . it's taken about five years. I think it needs to be like that because the human body is an incredibly complex piece of machinery. You need a real interest in science, but it's fascinating to study the human body in anatomy and physiology.

'I manage and treat sports injuries. First I assess a person's injury, then I need to provide a suitable management programme for my client . . . basically so they're doing the right things to heal themselves as efficiently as possible. I supervise exercise programmes and suggest gentle stretching techniques, and I carry out pre- and post-match massage for footballers.

'I do enjoy working with people, and I get to meet all sorts of people in the job. You sometimes need to be able to coax things out of them to get the right picture of what's happened. When you have a good knowledge of the injury and repair process you can get great pleasure in helping a sportsperson do what they need to do, to get better. It's a great feeling when you know you've done a good job.'

A vital part of a sports physio's job is not only treating injuries, but also helping athletes to recover quickly.

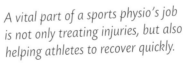

TO BECOME A SPORTS PHYSIOTHERAPIST, YOU WILL NEED

●

good communication skills

●

an interest in science, especially human biology

●

dexterity with your hands

TO BECOME A SPORTS PSYCHOLOGIST, YOU WILL NEED

- *good counselling skills*
- *powers of motivation*
- *problem-solving skills*

Sports scientists use sophisticated equipment to analyse an athlete's performance. Minor changes in approach can have huge benefits.

THE APPLIANCE OF SCIENCE

There is a very fine line between sporting success and failure, so it is not surprising that professional sportsmen and women turn to sport and exercise scientists to help with their performance and development.

SPORT AND EXERCISE SCIENTISTS

Sports scientists give players and athletes expert scientific support, working with other professionals such as technical coaches, physiotherapists, and nutritionists or dieticians. Exercise scientists help improve a sportsperson's health, for example after a bout of illness or injury. They work with the athlete through a highly focused programme of physical activity. Sport and exercise scientists have an in-depth knowledge of the human body's structure and function. They understand human physiology and the complex way in which the body responds to exercise and training. Part of their job is to analyse how the athlete's body moves during training and action. Armed with this information, the athlete can make minor adjustments to develop peak performance. Sport scientists may be employed by universities, sports clubs and sport institutes.

SPORTS PSYCHOLOGY

Sports psychologists can help sportsmen and women achieve more in their area of expertise by assessing and improving their mental and emotional state.

MAIN TASKS – SPORTS PSYCHOLOGIST

- *setting goals or targets for clients*
- *supporting clients in mental aspects*
- *discussing specific performances*
- *talking about personal issues*
- *helping to motivate clients*

Meera – sports psychologist

'I was a PE teacher initially and played a lot of hockey and squash and kept myself very fit, so I've always had that fundamental interest in physical education and sport. I'd also studied sports science and sports psychology at college, and I really loved the sports psychology aspect of my course.

Good sports psychologists may have the opportunity to work freelance or do special consultancy work.

'In my job as a sports psychologist I enjoy the close relationships you establish with sportsmen and women. They're usually very motivated, competitive individuals, but they're human . . . and, like everyone, they have their ups and downs. I'm there for them to talk to, and to work things out. They come to me to deal with any performance problems or personal issues that may have become a bit of a block. I try to help them achieve specific targets and goals. I also like working with other sports professionals – I tend to spend a lot of time with physiotherapists, coaches and other sports scientists.

'Sometimes I have to travel, so I'm away from home for longer than I'd like, but that can happen in any job . . . and the good bits far outweigh the parts I don't like.'

MAIN TASKS – SPORTS NUTRITIONIST

● *working with an athlete to achieve his/her aims*

● *considering an athlete's medical profile, body composition etc.*

● *assessing an athlete's diet*

● *checking hydration levels (urine/sweat)*

● *checking blood tests with a doctor*

● *working out an individual dietary programme*

YOU ARE WHAT YOU EAT

Sportsmen and women have to consider every aspect of their sporting performance, including the build-up to the event or match and the recovery period, as well as the rest of their everyday lives. Proper hydration and healthy eating can help athletes improve their stamina and performance. Sports nutritionists look closely at what athletes eat and drink so that they can help them improve their diet and maximise their performance.

SCIENTIFIC MINDS

A sports nutritionist needs an enquiring mind and must enjoy science, in particular chemistry. He or she will have an interest in human physiology and nutrition. Sports nutritionists advise athletes on good nutrition, working with fellow professionals such as coaches, doctors and lifestyle advisers to help sportsmen and women make the most of their individual talents.

Professional athletes like American footballer Marlin Jackson need a team of support staff. The sports nutritionist (on the far right) holds examples of foods that will improve his performance.

Dieticians and sports nutritionists will be aware of the importance of eating the right types of food to aid good health.

Sports nutritionists use specialist computer software packages to help analyse specific diets; they also use equipment such as body-mass scales. They usually work for professional clubs and sports institutes, as well as privately. Many professional players, athletes and sportspeople pursue other careers as well as their chosen sport, so nutritionists may need to be flexible enough to work with them at evenings and weekends.

DIETICIANS

Dieticians train to be experts in diet and nutrition. They often work in hospitals and health practices, advising people on eating more healthily and devising special diets for medical conditions such as diabetes. Some dieticians help to promote awareness of dietary health, while others specialise in sports, advising athletes on their diet. In this respect, their role begins to overlap with sports nutritionists. They can help players and athletes by working out all-important meals and drinks before and after sporting activity.

WHERE WILL I BE?
Professional sportsmen and women can earn enormous salaries, but their careers do not last very long. If they look after themselves and manage to avoid serious career-threatening injuries, they may continue at the top of their game for between ten and 15 years. Professionals should therefore think about a second career while they are still playing. Because they have an in-depth knowledge and overriding passion for their specialist sport, many ex-professionals choose to coach or become sporting consultants. Some become experts in various media, for example, on television, radio, or as newspaper sports columnists.

Leisure Centre Work

Leisure centre management, also known as sport and recreation facility management, involves running all aspects of leisure centres – from checking the water quality of a swimming pool to fixing an exercise bike or helping with first aid.

ACTIVE LEISURE

What we do when we are not working is our own business, but 'leisure' is one of our basic rights and it is essential for our proper functioning and well-being. Arts centres, theatres and theme parks are also to do with 'leisure', but this chapter is concerned with the matter of 'active leisure', and the special types of facilities we can visit to exercise or play sports. Leisure facilities can help fulfil a need for individuals and the community, and a well-run sports and leisure centre can be a very profitable venture. Typical places include leisure centres, health and fitness clubs and spas, as well as sports clubs.

These clients are taking part in a martial arts lesson in a modern leisure centre.

HANDY HINT
There are three levels of qualification in the sport and recreation sector. The Institute of Sport and Recreation Management (ISRM) has the following certificates: in operations, in supervisory management and the ISRM/ City & Guilds Higher Professional Diploma. You can study for both the operations and supervisory management certificates through work-based learning or via a full-time course. The diploma is available only to those in management positions within the sport and recreation sector.

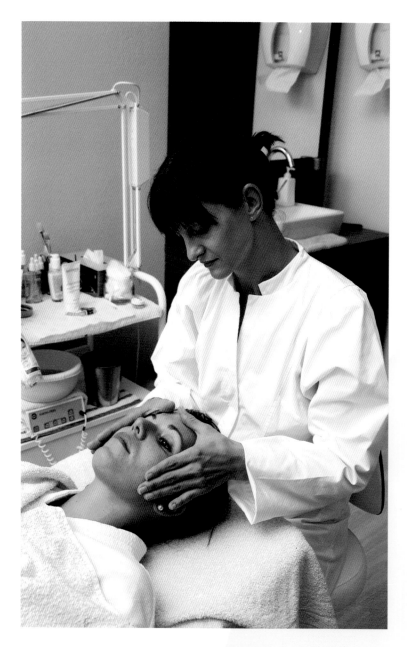

Larger leisure centres have extra facilities, such as health spas where beauticians and massage therapists can pamper clients.

PYRAMID STRUCTURE

Generally the leisure industry has a very broad-based pyramid structure, with considerably more jobs at a basic level than in senior positions. For example, on any one shift, depending on the size of a leisure centre's swimming pool, several attendants or assistants will need to work poolside. A supervisor will oversee the work of staff and the day-to-day activities of the centre. A large, complex leisure centre may employ an assistant manager as well as a leisure centre manager who is responsible for the management and motivation of staff, administration, financial management, marketing and promotion of the centre.

FINDING A JOB

If you want a job in this sector, you need to be resourceful and determined, as well as good at sports. If you live near a regularly patrolled stretch of coast, train as a lifeguard so you can work summer months – volunteer, if necessary. Contact all local leisure centres, fitness clubs, gyms, health farms and spas. Try to exhaust all possibilities, then cast your net wider to include other areas you could travel or move to. If you get an opportunity, grab it. Show willing, and agree to work less popular shifts as a leisure attendant. Your job will also involve cleaning showers, changing rooms and toilets. Demonstrate your willingness to work hard and your keenness to learn.

Donna – leisure centre manager

'I enjoy the variety of my job. On a Monday I might be preparing a weekly cash statement, working on spreadsheets and databases on the computer, and catching up on emails. Or I might be checking the temperature and the water chemical levels in the pool or the jacuzzi, dealing with customers, supervising staff, carrying out customer surveys or working out how to offer things to encourage more people to visit the leisure centre. You have to like meeting people, and I enjoy working with people.

'I left school and worked as a leisure centre attendant first. My boss encouraged me to go and study for a supervisory certificate, then a diploma. The extra skills and qualifications are useful in the job, because I can now do first aid, instruct or coach various classes like aqua-aerobics and swimming or train pool lifeguards, as well as run the leisure centre. I accept the complaints that customers might have, as that's part of the job too.

From gym instructors to lifeguards, the job of a leisure centre manager is to encourage good relations among members of the staff team.

'I'd prefer to do this job than be stuck behind a desk all day. You have to be a bit of a jack-of-all-trades – I've been duty manager here for 11 years and it's great for the variety every day.'

TO BECOME A LEISURE CENTRE MANAGER, YOU WILL NEED

•

an interest in sport and exercise

•

good 'people skills'

•

excellent organisational skills

WHAT'S ON OFFER?

From day to day, sports facility or leisure centre managers may have quite different jobs depending on the size of the centre and the services they offer. A small community leisure centre, for example, may offer a standard rectangular swimming pool with a separate toddler and baby pool and a gym. A more upmarket version in a modern structure could provide curved pools with slides, wave machines, a fitness suite, a beauty spa, squash courts, indoor pitches for five-a-side football, racquet sports and gymnastics, together with a café and bar for customers. Leisure centre managers make sure the whole range of services and activities runs smoothly.

RUNNING THE SHOW

A leisure centre manager is on call to deal with troubleshooting, working quickly and efficiently to sort out any problems that may suddenly arise. The manager may have to drop everything to provide immediate first aid to someone in trouble, or to clear debris from the swimming pool. Leisure centre managers usually spend a lot of time on paperwork, such as filling in accident reports or invoices, as well as liaising with staff to sort out minor everyday matters. A good manager will always have an eye to the future – planning, developing and structuring new services for the public.

Modern leisure centres may contain swimming pools with recreation as well as fitness in mind. These are often equipped with slides, jacuzzis, wave machines and lounging areas.

MAIN TASKS – LEISURE CENTRE MANAGER

•

running the centre and supervising staff

•

maintaining the swimming pool

•

maintaining health and safety

•

doing administrative and financial tasks

•

using ICT for spreadsheets and databases

•

working out the timetable of the centre

•

promoting and marketing the centre

Leisure attendants can gain further qualifications while working, such as the ability to teach swimming classes.

Steve – leisure attendant

'For years I'd been doing triathlons – swimming, cycling and running events – and I happened upon the job because of some people I met for swim training. One of the girls I knew was a trainer at the local leisure centre. I started off part-time because of all the training I was doing for triathlons, but I work full-time here now.

'The variety of the job is good for me. I might be doing an induction for the gym, or taking a bike class, or I could be poolside watching the swimmers. There's a natural variety from Monday to Friday, then the weekend – classes and clubs like toddler gym are booked in – but every day's different anyway. You get to know the people who come in to exercise, and there's a good mix of customers. Sometimes more serious things can happen . . . it might be very quiet one day, then, if someone has a heart attack, you have to switch suddenly and act quickly and calmly – do first aid or call for help or emergency services. You need to use your own initiative at times like this. You're never stuck doing the same thing in this job, that's for sure.'

TO BECOME A LEISURE ATTENDANT, YOU WILL NEED

●

an outgoing personality

●

a cool head in an emergency

●

the ability to work as part of a team

Leisure attendants may choose to attend courses to become qualified gym instructors.

BASIC DUTIES

Leisure attendants in health clubs or leisure centres will have a variety of duties in their work. No matter what the size of the organisation, general everyday tasks will probably involve reception work (providing information about activities and taking payments), cleaning and tidying rotas, patrolling and looking out for potential health and safety risks.

Leisure attendants may be responsible for specific areas, and it will be up to them to plan and prepare for certain activities at set times. For example, a leisure attendant may need to get a court or pitch ready for a badminton competition for one hour, followed by a children's party, then football. It will be the leisure attendant's responsibility to set up, maintain and demonstrate equipment. He or she will also supervise facility users, checking that customers make use of the equipment safely.

WORKING SHIFTS

Health or sports clubs and leisure centres try to offer customers the widest possible range of facilities and services. This often means extended opening hours to cater for working adults. As a result, leisure attendants are likely to have early shifts, starting from 7am, and afternoon shifts running through to as late as 11pm. Weekend shifts will also be a regular feature.

MAIN TASKS – LEISURE ATTENDANT

●

carrying out reception work

●

cleaning and patrolling the building

●

dealing with first aid incidents

●

supervising gym and induction classes

●

taking swimming and exercise classes

LIFEGUARDS AND POOL ATTENDANTS

Whether you want to work indoors or outdoors, at a pool or on the beach, you will only be able to work as a pool or beach lifeguard if you obtain the necessary lifesaving qualifications. Most leisure centres will let you train on the job.

SAFETY FIRST

Lifeguards are responsible for making sure members of the public are safe in and near water. Weak swimmers can suddenly find themselves out of their depth, so that they panic, and even confident swimmers can get into difficulty in lakes and especially in the sea, where there are strong currents and hidden rocks.

Beach and pool lifeguards need to be physically fit, and strong swimmers. They must be diligent and observant in their duties, and able to concentrate, without getting distracted easily by the noise and movement of people having fun around them. They need to be able to anticipate danger, and act calmly, quickly and decisively if there is a problem or emergency. Pool lifeguards must be at least 16 years old, while beach lifeguards must be 18 years old or more.

WHERE WILL I BE?
If you're interested in physical fitness, sports and exercise, you may want to run your own leisure centre in the future. Find some work in a leisure centre to get some useful experience. You can progress from leisure attendant to supervisor, then to assistant manager. Ultimately you could become a leisure centre manager, or even an area manager or operations coordinator.

Becoming a lifeguard may seem very glamorous, but it is important to realise the responsibilities that come with the job.

Lifeguards keep a close eye on people in the pool. They may sometimes need to give immediate first aid.

Kelly – lifeguard

'I've always been a good swimmer, but there's a lot more to the job than just that. I've worked in indoor pools and outdoor pools and helped supervise beaches too. I'd say the main thing is to always be aware and on the lookout for something, just in case someone suddenly gets into trouble. I suppose it's easier keeping watch over a pool indoors, as it's a contained space, but if it's really busy then you've got to keep your wits about you all the time.

'It could be a weaker swimmer getting out of their depth, or people mucking about in the diving pool – you can get really serious spinal injuries if you're not careful on the diving boards. We tend to receive good training as a lifeguard, so ever since I've been working I've known to look out for the danger signs. I'm not afraid to raise my voice to get someone to listen . . . when it's in their own safety interests, of course!

'You'd be surprised how many people start getting worked up sometimes, so it's also important to know how to talk to people in the right way. I've learnt that on the job I suppose, and that's good, because I really like dealing with people on the whole.'

The Great Outdoors

One growing sub-sector of 'active leisure' is the area of outdoor recreation. The excitement of more adventurous activities, such as abseiling, climbing, mountain biking, horse-riding, sailing or canoeing is proving increasingly popular for young people and adults.

OUTDOOR ACTIVITIES OFFICERS

Outdoor activities officers may be known by many different titles – including outdoor education officers and outward-bound instructors – but they generally provide the same sort of services. They lead groups in a wide range of outdoor activities, from archery to windsurfing and abseiling to rock-climbing. Groups of children, young people and adults learn new skills as they participate in the activities. The instructors are there to make sure that people find out more about themselves – away from home, in a different setting, individuals have to work together as a team in a particular activity. For some participants it can be an emotional journey, but skilled instructors make the experience an enjoyable and memorable one for most people.

TO BECOME AN OUTDOOR ACTIVITIES OFFICER, YOU WILL NEED

●

good 'people skills'

●

leadership and teamwork skills

●

stamina and a love of the outdoors

MAIN TASKS – OUTDOOR ACTIVITIES OFFICER

●

planning, organising and carrying out activities

●

giving practical demonstrations and advice

●

maintaining and checking equipment carefully

●

ensuring the health and safety of individuals

●

assessing all hazards and managing risks

●

motivating individuals and teams

It is great to be out in the sun having fun during the summer holidays. Outdoor activity officers are there to make sure everyone has an enjoyable and safe time.

Before these young people try their hands at abseiling, they have their equipment checked carefully by an outdoor activities officer.

Jerzy – outdoor activities officer

'The best thing has got to be working outdoors, in stunning locations. I've always loved spending time hill-walking or trekking, climbing rocks and mountains, kayaking . . . solitary pursuits mainly. More recently I've had great fun in team pursuits, and this is especially true in what I do for a living. The outdoor activities business is a wonderful opportunity for different people to come together and enjoy themselves in beautiful surroundings.

'We do team-building for adults – companies might send their managers away for a few days and we arrange a series of activities which can be pretty competitive in nature, or alternatively they might be quite challenging for certain individuals. Everyone's different, so what's easy for one person can be a real challenge for others. It might be a matter of encouraging someone who's afraid of heights to abseil off a cliff or a huge bridge. I really enjoy seeing people having the time of their lives with us – one minute they're scared stiff, the next they're buzzing, saying: 'Can I have another go?'. I love working with children because they tell you honestly how great the experience is. Adults are good too – they turn into big kids when they are trying something new!

'The downside is that you're only working half of the year. You need another job, or other interests to keep you going during the winter. But that is the only downside.'

SAFE FROM HARM

In their work, outdoor activities officers provide many exciting experiences for others. However, they must plan everything carefully so that each separate group is catered for, taking into account all individual needs, as well as varying outdoor conditions. For example, heavy rainfall can make the activity of white-water rafting down a fast-flowing river too dangerous to undertake. Likewise, activities that are suitable for dry, sunny weather may have to be postponed if there are freezing blizzard conditions or gales. Instructors may also decide to adapt a programme slightly if there is a group of disabled individuals, or a number of people with very mixed abilities.

EXTREME SPORTS

Extreme sports are certain activities perceived as having a high level of risk. Extreme sports could include some of the outdoor activities already mentioned, but there are many more, and these 'sports' tend to be more concerned with thrill-seeking sensations than with team building. For example, if you want to supervise aerobatic flying, bungee jumping, canyoning, hovercrafting, coasteering, kitesurfing, land yachting or microliting, you are clearly interested in extreme sports! You will need to have nerves of steel, plenty of experience and determination – and you will of course need to be an extreme sports fanatic to stand any chance of landing a job in this highly competitive field.

WHERE WILL I BE?
If you love the great outdoors, then a career as an outdoor activities officer could be the one for you. If you start out as an outdoor activities officer or outdoor education officer you can move up to work as an outward-bound centre manager. From there you could set up your own business, providing outdoor activities or working for an outdoor education advisory committee.

Skydiving is a breathtaking activity. Future teachers will need a number of skydiving qualifications in order to teach groups.

Competition is fierce for jobs teaching extreme sports, such as bungee jumping. With these activities, safety is always the number one priority.

HORSE LOVERS ONLY

Riding centre managers must have a real passion for horses and ponies. They will need to work extremely hard to make a success of the business, and they will need to have plenty of previous experience in equestrian training and work. It is normal to start in a related job, such as that of horse groom, riding instructor or ride leader, before gaining suitable equestrian qualifications and working your way up into management. More experienced riding centre managers may wish to consider setting up their own businesses, for example providing accommodation as well as trekking and riding.

GROOMS AND RIDING INSTRUCTORS

Budding riding centre managers would do well to start work as horse grooms and riding instructors. Grooms look after horses and ponies on a daily basis, mucking out stables and cleaning the yard, leading the horses to the fields and keeping the animals clean and fed. Riding instructors teach a wide range of people to ride and devise training programmes so that individuals of different abilities develop their riding skills. In addition, instructors often also help groom horses and clean stables. Grooms and instructors need good stamina and must be able to ride well, and have a genuine interest in horses and their welfare.

FINDING A JOB
If you love horses and are planning to become a groom, you may well have already joined a pony club or riding school, and will be aware of all the local riding centres in your area. If you are riding well, ask the centre manager if there are any job opportunities. Let him or her know that you are really keen, and offer to work on a voluntary basis. In time you may be able to take an apprenticeship as a groom or riding instructor (though trainee instructors will need to get appropriate riding qualifications).

Riding holiday centres offer pony trekking across open countryside. Some pony treks are in stunning locations.

MAIN TASKS – RIDING CENTRE MANAGER

• *organising and leading treks*

• *looking after the health and welfare of horses*

• *looking after customers*

• *running and promoting the business*

• *supervising staff*

• *looking after the facilities at the centre*

Alexandra – riding centre manager

'I've loved horses for as long as I can remember. I had a favourite pony when I was about four, and I learnt to ride when I was very young. You definitely need that total passion for horses in the first place for this job. I've got it and I think most of the girls riding here have got it too.

'Although it's a great job, you do need to work really hard. You're outside a lot, so the weather's not always sunny and dry. I regularly come back home soaked to the skin. It's a business, and we're lucky to have the farm here too. It's taken quite a few years for the horse-riding to take off, but we're doing OK now. I have to be on call all the time, as I live right next door to the centre. I do tend to work very long hours, including weekends and evenings, so that can rule out a social life. But the people who come to ride with us love coming here and a lot of them come back, so it's a bit like seeing old friends sometimes. You need to like people, but the most important thing is a love of horses. That makes it the best job in the world.'

Grooms and riding centre managers work hard looking after the horses, but the job is a real passion.

TO BECOME A RIDING CENTRE MANAGER, YOU WILL NEED

●

good riding skills

●

a love of horses

●

good leadership skills

Sport and Leisure Tuition

The growing interest in sport and leisure is reflected in coaching, instructing and teaching roles. A sports coach can instruct teams or individuals, children or adults, amateurs or professionals. He or she will often teach or instruct a specific sport or interest.

Sports coaches must have a recognised teaching qualification. Tennis coaches spend lots of time teaching one-to-one.

GROUPS OR ONE-TO-ONE

Today there are opportunities for teaching a huge range of sporting and leisure activities. Many people wish to increase their fitness levels for health and well-being, and start by joining a gym. After a short induction, gym members can usually train alone and require minimum supervision. However, other people may prefer to concentrate on learning a sport, martial art or skill, and will require coaches and instructors to provide group lessons or classes, or one-to-one tuition.

PART-TIME OR FULL-TIME

Many coaches teach part-time, or on a voluntary basis, so need a second career in addition to coaching. There are opportunities as self-employed coaches. Full-time coaches may have built up a good reputation after a successful sporting career and be recognised as an authority in their chosen field. Instructors and coaches work in a variety of settings, from local sports clubs to national teams, and from youth clubs to community leisure centres and private health clubs.

TO BECOME A SPORTS COACH, YOU WILL NEED

●

enthusiasm

●

initiative

●

a love of sport and physical activity

Whatever the sport, coaches need to support and motivate athletes. They need an in-depth knowledge too.

Matt – sports coach

'I find that building relationships and working with children and young people, seeing them learn and develop and providing a fun activity is one of the most rewarding things I have experienced. A lot of young people from around here come from a difficult background, and to know that you make a difference, even a small one, makes the job thoroughly rewarding. The team we work with is very enthusiastic, and passionate about sport and healthy, active living . . . to be a part of this group is something I enjoy. Even on a difficult day, I get to deliver sport and physical activity to children in a fun, learning environment.

'Sometimes full-time coaching posts can be hard to come by, but I started off working part-time for a coaching company. That helped me get this job as a senior sports coach, managing a team of community sports coaches for a range of different activities. My role also entails creating, maintaining and strengthening links between schools and various sports clubs.

'I find I have to strike the correct balance in my job between sports coaching and keeping up to date with planning and paperwork. My role this year has more involvement in management, so I have a lot of responsibility and need to get into the office more often. But I enjoy the coaching side of the job best.'

*Rock climbing
instructors build up beginners'
confidence on indoor equipment
before letting them try difficult outdoor climbs.*

INDOOR AND OUTDOOR ACTIVITIES

Popular indoor activities that need competent coaches and instructors in leisure centres and sports clubs include swimming, squash, badminton, trampolining, ice skating and indoor climbing. There is also a great range of martial arts available, from judo to karate and from aikido to taekwondo. Children and adults can progress by achieving different belts and levels. Coaches can be in greater demand throughout the summer months, teaching more activities outdoors such as tennis, cricket and golf.

GETTING THE BEST

Instruction demands great technical skill in particular sports. It is equally important that the coach is able to communicate effectively. A learner will need to respect the instructor and will probably enjoy classes more and learn more quickly if he or she likes the person too. A coach needs to know exactly when to encourage an individual or the whole team, and when to increase the pressure or demands and talk tough. Coaches may have to work with a wide range of abilities, and will therefore need powers of patience and tact to inspire and motivate so that they get the best from their students.

HANDY HINT

You will need an approved national qualification, such as an NVQ or SVQ, to become a personal trainer or health and fitness instructor. You will then qualify to hold current insurance and become a member of the Register of Exercise Professionals. Further qualifications, such as the Fitness Leaders' Certificate from the ISRM (Institute of Sport and Recreation Management) will enhance your prospects of promotion if you work for an organisation such as a leisure centre.

HEALTH AND FITNESS INSTRUCTORS

Health and fitness instructors may take a variety of classes in private gyms, health clubs, leisure centres and community halls. Many are qualified to take all types of group exercise classes and health activities such as aerobic workouts, circuit training, yoga or Pilates classes. Some will also give one-to-one instruction.

EXERCISE ROUTINES

A health and fitness instructor will work out an exercise routine that is suitable for the abilities and stamina of each class. For example, instructors may offer classes for older people that will concentrate on stretching and gentle movements, and will provide some fun for those wishing to maintain a little independence in their lives rather than indulge in an energetic workout. Instructors will want to incorporate their own interests into a group exercise workout. This may include playing disco or dance music to provide a lively background for exercising. Many will also wish to use suitable equipment to vary routines – this may include using mats, weights and steps.

TO BECOME A HEALTH AND FITNESS INSTRUCTOR, YOU WILL NEED

●

a good level of physical fitness

●

enthusiasm and a lively nature

●

excellent communication skills

Most Pilates or yoga teachers are self-employed. They often work in health clubs and sports centres to start to build up classes.

Shara – personal trainer

'It's not like I rush into work every day, but I do really enjoy the job. In fact it's great being able to turn an interest, or with me a bit of an obsession, into a profession. I liked playing sports at first, but moved away from team sports like hockey and started going down to the gym a lot more . . . running on the treadmill, working out, swimming and generally keeping fit. I worked really hard on my own fitness as a teenager. I was leaving school but didn't really know what to do for a career. I had a couple of part-time jobs, but that was when I realised I'd be a lot happier working at the gym.

'It's hard work and you need to do long hours to succeed. It's very important to motivate others. Sometimes people think they want to get fit, lose weight and eat more healthily, but they lack the will-power. That can be frustrating, when people give up so quickly. Even harder is when they're doing quite well, but progress is gradual and they want a miracle cure . . . and they stop coming to see me. My thing is to always give them realistic goals.'

Instructors can provide group exercise classes, for example aerobics, which can be a lot of fun as well as a good workout.

Personal trainers can help people to exercise in a safe and effective way. They can give advice on gym equipment.

KEEPING IT SAFE

Health and fitness instructors, including personal trainers, help people to exercise in a safe environment. All individuals have different needs and the instructor will need to be very aware of disabilities, as well as the sort of less visible injuries or ongoing conditions, such as back problems, that people may have. Some people may be overweight or obese, others may be involved in rehabilitation or recovering from injury, while others may not have exercised for many years. The instructor will need to carry out an initial assessment of individuals before they are able to participate. A gym instructor, for example, will carry out an induction class for gym members before allowing them to use complicated lifting equipment and exercise machines. Good instructors will understand the human body and decide how best to modify training programmes to allow for people with different types of health problems or injuries.

KEEPING UP TO DATE

Fitness instructors will need to keep up-to-date with developments in exercise equipment and fitness regimes. In this way they will be able to provide customers with the best in the latest exercise techniques. Many health and fitness instructors work part-time or as freelances. A successful instructor will need to be flexible and resourceful, often working from more than one health club or fitness suite. He or she will also need to think of new opportunities and ways to promote the business and stay ahead of the competition.

MAIN TASKS – HEALTH AND FITNESS INSTRUCTOR

●

assessing and inducting new members

●

making individual training programmes

●

writing class programmes

●

providing advice on lifestyle and nutrition

●

keeping up to date with equipment and techniques

PE teachers spend most of their time delivering an active programme of sports. They also use ICT to investigate their subject and for student tracking.

PE TEACHERS

There are many different professional roles for those interested in the benefits of physical education and exercise. Physical education officers can work within the prison service, providing exercise assistance and classes for inmates and prisoners. Officers in the armed forces may decide to specialise in physical education so that they can provide sports and training for men and women. Most physical education teachers have a specialised role within education and deliver an essential active programme of exercise and sports. They give training to children and young people in specialist colleges and schools within the curriculum, as well as a range of extra-curricular sporting activities, such as football coaching skills, athletics and tennis tuition.

WHERE WILL I BE?

If you have a particular sporting skill and are interested in a career as a sports coach, one of the routes you might be able to take is to start as a good amateur player, then progress from there to volunteer coach, and then to part-time and ultimately full-time coach. You may continue on this career ladder to become a senior sports coach or a manager of community sports coaches.

MAIN TASKS – PE TEACHER

●

encouraging pupils to attain individual goals

●

developing personalised plans for pupils

●

assessing, tracking and recording pupil progress

●

providing out-of-hours opportunities for pupils

●

managing staff

●

providing positive experiences for pupils

●

using ICT for assessment and following the curriculum

Ben – physical education teacher

'My own love of sport at school as a child, and what I did outside of school in football, athletics, climbing and outdoor pursuits with family and friends, left a mark on me. This enjoyment and feeling of freedom from 'normal' everyday experiences played a big part in my life from school through to university. The idea of keeping fit and healthy while enjoying yourself seemed the perfect way to earn a living . . . so I studied PE and sport at university and my career began from there.

'The most difficult parts of the job are paperwork and challenging pupils, with whom we are supposed to deliver the perfect lesson. This can be hard sometimes, but I do really enjoy the job. I love trying to motivate young people to understand and enjoy sport and physical activity. Most rewarding is seeing young people realise their potential in sport and become more confident about themselves. I enjoy working outside of a normal classroom, in a sports hall or on a mountain. This helps to bring variety to my role. Whether it is a promising athlete reaching county standard or an overweight pupil with lesser abilities becoming interested in their physical fitness and skill development – they are both rewarding and enjoyable aspects of the job.'

A good PE teacher can help to build students' physical confidence.

Sport and Leisure Development

Many governments around the world are focusing on the development of the sport and leisure industry. By improving this sector, countries can gain considerable status through their sporting achievements in various world cups and tournaments, and provide healthy opportunities for everyone to enjoy their leisure time.

A SPORTING CULTURE

World cups and sporting tournaments, such as the Olympics and Paralympics, are the height of sporting culture and achievement. When countries host these prestigious events, a hugely complex infrastructure is put in place – town planners create new Olympic villages to include stadia and arenas, hotel accommodation, railway stations, car parks, food venues and so on.

People competing, helping to organise or simply watching the Olympic Games are all part of a wonderful showcase of sport.

FINDING A JOB

If you want a job as a sports development officer, it is important to be inquisitive and knowledgeable. Find out as much as you can about the changing world of sport and leisure development and sporting opportunities. You may want to work towards a suitable sporting degree. Once qualified, you will need to contact your local authority – their website will list all such jobs. Local authorities also advertise in local and national newspapers.

We all need to take responsibility for our well-being. Understanding how important it is to be fit and healthy is a good place to start.

GLOBALISATION

In recent years, globalisation has meant an increase in cooperation between nations in many areas – politically, economically and culturally. This cooperation has extended to leisure activities. Sport can send out a positive message that national barriers and obstacles can be removed and that healthy sporting endeavour is a worthwhile and potentially unifying force. Significantly, sport is also big business – golfer Tiger Woods and football player David Beckham are no longer simply sportsmen, they have become sporting 'brands'.

GET FIT

Sports development is important, not just for top-quality sports but for society in general. As the modern-day couch-potato culture keeps millions in its grip and obesity figures continue to rise, it is necessary to improve the overall health of most nations. If more people exercise, get fit and play sports, then fewer people run the risk of dying prematurely of heart disease or other diet-related illnesses. Sports development is all about providing opportunities for the good of everyone.

MAIN TASKS – SPORTS DEVELOPMENT OFFICER

●

organising activities for different sports

●

helping and supporting sports clubs or organisations

●

organising sports events and competitions

●

identifying and accessing appropriate sources of funding

●

supporting and developing coaches

●

working with different partners to promote sport

LINKS AND PARTNERSHIPS

Sports development officers (SDOs) try to make sure people of all ages and abilities have the chance to take part in various sports, develop their skills in the sport of their choice, and lead a healthy lifestyle. Officers work with their local community, organising volunteers and helping groups gain funding and grants. They liaise with local groups and schools, as well as national governing bodies for individual sports. To develop positive sporting opportunities for everyone, sporting bodies and organisations need to function efficiently on a local, regional and national level, creating links and lasting partnerships with communities, schools and clubs.

COMMUNITY SPORTS

Sports development officers work in a team to promote and develop sport and leisure activities for all sections of the community. Community SDOs may work closely with education welfare officers and the police, as they try to promote all types of sport projects for groups of young people such as school truants or youth offenders. Such projects can be very successful in more deprived areas, getting youths involved in positive, enjoyable sporting events.

SPECIFIC SPORTS

Some SDOs promote a specific sport, such as tennis, hockey or athletics. Their job is to endeavour to make the right opportunities available for people to take part in and compete in their chosen sport at the appropriate level.

TO BECOME A SPORTS DEVELOPMENT OFFICER, YOU WILL NEED

●

enthusiasm, passion and motivation

●

good communication skills

●

initiative and flexibility

Sports development officers help provide people of all ages and skills with the opportunity to enjoy playing sport.

Clubs in the local community can give people new sporting or leisure experiences. Some find a skill for life.

Amy – sports development officer

'I was originally looking at going into rehabilitation. My local hospital had directed me to an exercise referral scheme and I contacted them about work experience and found that the scheme was part of a sports development team. I did a six-week placement as part of my degree and ended up working alongside the sports development officer, where I became really interested in sports development.

'I like seeing people have positive experiences in sport and physical activity. It's really good when you have helped a group, club or school to achieve something really positive.

'Sometimes there can be a lot of paperwork involved and it can be hard to chase people for this . . . there just isn't enough time to do all the things you would like. Having quite a wide remit, sometimes I have to spread myself thinly instead of spending more time on certain worthwhile projects. When arranging different sporting sessions or activities, you may not be sure what the response will be, so when there is a good number of participants and they enjoy themselves, it makes everything worthwhile. It's also satisfying to help give support and funding for projects or clubs and see it being put to good use. We want to provide as many opportunities for sport as possible in the local area.'

SPORTS FOR ALL

One important area of growth within sport and leisure is the provision of opportunities for disabled people. Sporting organisations and bodies now look at their policies and programmes with an awareness of including more disabled people. This can be as an inclusive facility within the existing sporting programme or to provide dedicated sporting opportunities, such as wheelchair tennis and basketball, restricted to disabled sportsmen and women.

DISABILITY SPORTS DEVELOPMENT OFFICERS

A disability sports development officer will work with various national governing bodies of individual sports to provide and develop more sporting opportunities for disabled people. The officer's focus may be national and regional, as well as local. Officers arrange meetings with appropriate sporting bodies, help with their development plans for disabled competitors and identify suitable clubs for sports. They may make presentations to groups and provide advice on inclusion issues, helping disabled people to find somewhere to play sports, train or exercise.

MAIN TASKS – DISABILITY SPORTS DEVELOPMENT OFFICER

●

ensuring that disability sports are available

●

setting up meetings

●

assisting sporting bodies with development plans

●

providing advice on inclusion issues

●

showing people a range of sporting opportunities

●

looking at coaching strategies

●

helping people to play in competitions

TO BECOME A DISABILITY SPORTS DEVELOPMENT OFFICER, YOU WILL NEED

●

good communication skills

●

the ability to work in a team

●

knowledge of sports development

Helping disabled people compete in sports is rewarding, but sports development officers also need to keep lots of people involved.

With proper facilities, coaching and support, disabled athletes can train to compete for the Paralympics.

Catherine – disability sports development officer

'While studying for my Sport and Recreation Management degree I had many work placements, delivering sporting activities to both disabled young people and adults.

'In my job I have the opportunity to meet lots of different people from different backgrounds . . . I then work with these people to see how we can move disability sport forward. I really enjoy the partnership and networking of this post. It allows me to be a part of many exciting developments. You have to be a 'people person' and enjoy the challenges that this type of work brings. I have great passion and drive and I enjoy the variety of the job.

'At present there is only one disability sports development officer in the county and that person is me! This means that I have many priorities across many different areas of work including coaching, volunteers, competitions and festivals, clubs, physical activity and inclusive fitness initiative. I try to build capacity in all of these areas so that I empower other people to develop sport for disabled people.

'I have to work very hard to convince people that, firstly, they should be providing opportunities for disabled people and, secondly, that disabled people should be treated as any other person. They should be respected and they deserve the right to be able to access sports activities, like anyone else in this world.'

Further Information

BOOKS

Gray, Philip **The Penguin Careers Guide**, Penguin, 2008

Griffin, Murray and Philip Watkins **Sport and Exercise Science: An Introduction**, Hodder Arnold, 2005

Hodgson, Susan (ed.) **A-Z of Careers and Jobs**, Kogan Page, 2008

Long, Dr Jonathan A. **Researching Leisure, Sport and Tourism**, Sage Publications Ltd, 2007

Lore, Nicholas and Anthony Spadafore **Now What? The Young Person's Guide to Choosing the Perfect Career**, Fireside Books, 2008

McMahon-Beattie, Una and Ian Yeoman **Sport and Leisure Operations Management**, Thomson Learning, 2004

WEBSITES

http://careersadvice.direct.gov.uk/helpwithyourcareer/jobprofiles/
Search through the range of professions within the 'Sport, Leisure and Tourism' directory.

www.alec.co.uk
A website with general advice and information on careers. Includes tips on writing a CV, finding a job and handling an interview.

www.careers-guide.com/industry-choices/sport-leisure.htm
General information with advice on sport and leisure careers including sport scientist, sport psychologist and fitness instructor.

www.connexions-direct.com/
A website with invaluable information and advice for young people, including a useful database of professions (jobs4u) within 'job families'.

www.leisurejobs.com
Browse this careers' website to see what sort of jobs are on offer at entry level.

Glossary

abseiling descending a vertical surface, such as a rock or cliff, using a rope coiled around the body

active leisure activities that involve the exertion of physical energy

administrative to do with administration, or dealing with business matters

aerobic exercise an activity such as swimming or running that increases the efficiency of oxygen intake by the lungs and heart for the working muscles (it usually involves constant moderate-intensity exercise)

body composition the way in which a person's body is made up

counselling skills the ability to help clients by listening and talking

debris rubbish or litter

disabled lacking one or more physical powers, such as the ability to walk

equestrian to do with horses or riding

freelance a self-employed person who does work for various employers

globalisation the interconnection of economic, political and cultural activities across the world

hydration adding water to restore or maintain correct fluid balance

inclusion being included, for example, through the provision of sporting activities for all ages and abilities

induction classes classes where people are formally introduced by an expert, for example, to special equipment in a gym

manipulation treating manually, for example, by using the hands during massage therapy

martial arts various forms of self-defence, such as judo, used for exercise, in competition and for self-protection

nutrition a science that deals with food and nourishment, especially in humans

Olympics short for Olympic Games, a multi-sport event held every four years for able-bodied athletes

Paralympics short for Paralympic Games, a multi-sport event held every four years for athletes with disabilities

physiology the study of the way in which living organisms and their parts function

Pilates an exercise system based on aerobics and yoga, building strength without muscle bulk

prematurely unexpectedly early

psychology the study of all forms of behaviour

recreation an activity done for relaxation or pleasure

rehabilitation helping a patient get better, for example, when a sportsperson recovers from injury

remit an area of responsibility or expertise

replica tops sport shirts similar to those worn by professionals, for example, football tops

stamina endurance, resistance to fatigue

supervisory to do with someone who supervises or manages

talent scout someone who is employed to seek out and recognise skilled or gifted individuals

Index

Numbers in **bold** refer to illustrations

active leisure 6, 7, **7**, 6, **16**, 24, **32**, 38, **39**
administration 6, 7, 17, 19
aerobics teacher 18, 34
agent 8
armed forces, working in 36

beautician 17, **17**

coaching 7, 12, 13, 14, 15, 18, 27, 30-31, **30–31**, 32, 36, 39, 42, 43
communication 7, 10, 11, 12, 13, 18, 19, 23, 32, 33, 40, 42
community 16, 19, 30, 31, 33, 36, 40, 41

dietician 12, 15
disability sports development officer 42–43
disabled athletes 8, 26, 42, 43, **42**, **43**

equipment **7**, 12, 15, 21, 24, 25, 32, 33, 35
extreme sports 26–27, **26–27**

fitness suite 19, 35
football 7, 8, 9, **9**, 11, 19, 21, 36, 37, 39
footballer 8–9, 11, 39

globalisation 39
golfing caddy 8
groundsperson 8
gym instructor 35
gyms 7, **7**, 17, **18**, 19, 20, 21, **21**, 30, 33, 34, 35

health and fitness 6, 7, 9, 10, 13, 16, 17, 19, 22, 30, 32, 33, 34, 35, 37, 39, 43
health and fitness clubs 10, 16, 17, 21, 30, 33, 41, 43
health and fitness instructor 32, 33, 34, 35
health and safety 19, 21, 22, 23, 24, 26, 27, 35
health spas 16, 17, 19
horse groom 27, 28, 29
horse riding 7, 24, 27–29, **28–29**
horse riding centre manager 27-29
hospitals and health practices, working in 15

inclusion 40, 42
induction classes 20, 21, 30, 35
Institute of Sport and Recreation Management (ISRM) 16, 32

job satisfaction 9, 11, 13, 18, 20, 23, 25, 29, 31, 34, 37, 41, 43

leadership 7, 24, 27, 29, 32
leisure attendant 17, 18, 20–21, **20–21**, 22
leisure centre assistant manager 17, 22
leisure centre manager 16, 17, 18–19, **18**, 22
leisure centre supervisor 16, 17, 18, 22
leisure centres 7, 10, 16–23, **16**, **19**, 30, 32, 33
lifeguard 17, 18, 21, 22–23, **22–23**

martial arts 30, 32
massage therapy 10, 11, 17
motivation 7, 10, 12, 13, 17, 24, 31, 32, 34, 37, 40

Olympics 38, **38**
outdoor activities 6, 7, 24–30, **24–25**, 32, 37
outdoor activities officer 24-27, **24–25**
outdoor education officer 24 (see also outdoor activities officer)
outward bound centre manager 26
outward bound instructor 24 (see also outdoor activities officer)

Paralympics 8, 38, 43
PE teacher 13, 36–37, **36–37**
peak performance 10, 12
personal trainer 32, 34, 35, **34**, **35** (see also health and fitness instructor)
physical education officer 36
physiology 11, 12, 14
Pilates instructor 33, **33**
pool attendant 22 (see also lifeguard)
pony club 28 (see also horse riding)
prisons, working in 36
professional sportspeople 7, 8, 10, 11, 12, 13, 14, **14**, 15, 39, 42

qualifications 16, 18, 20, 22, 26, 27, 28, 30, 32, 33, 38, 39

reception work 21
referee 8
ride leader 27
riding instructor 27, 28
rock climbing instructor **32**

science 11, 12, 13, 14
sport and leisure development 38–43
sport and leisure tuition 30–37, **30–31**

sport and recreation facility (see leisure centre)
sports clubs 7, 10, 12, 14, 15, 16, 21, 30, 31, 32, 39, 40, 41, 42, 43
sports coach 30–31, 36
sports development officer (SDO) 7, 39–43, **41**
sports institutes, working in 15
sports nutritionist 12, 14–15, **14**
sports physiotherapist 10–11, **10–11**, 12, 13
sports psychologist 12–13, **13**
sports promotion 7, 17, 39
sports science 12, **12**, 13
stable hand 8
swimming pool **6**, 16, 17, 18, 19, **19**, 20, **20**, 21, 23

talent scout 8
teams and teamwork 7, 8, 9, 14, 18, 21, 24, 25, 26, 30, 31, 32, 34, 40, 41, 42
tennis 7, 8, **8**, **10**, 30, 32, 36, 40, **40**, 42
trekking 7, 25, 27, 28

umpire 8

voluntary work 17, 18, 30 36, 40, 43

yoga instructor **33**